Octo's Coral Reef

Written and illustrated by Elisa B. Karnofsky.

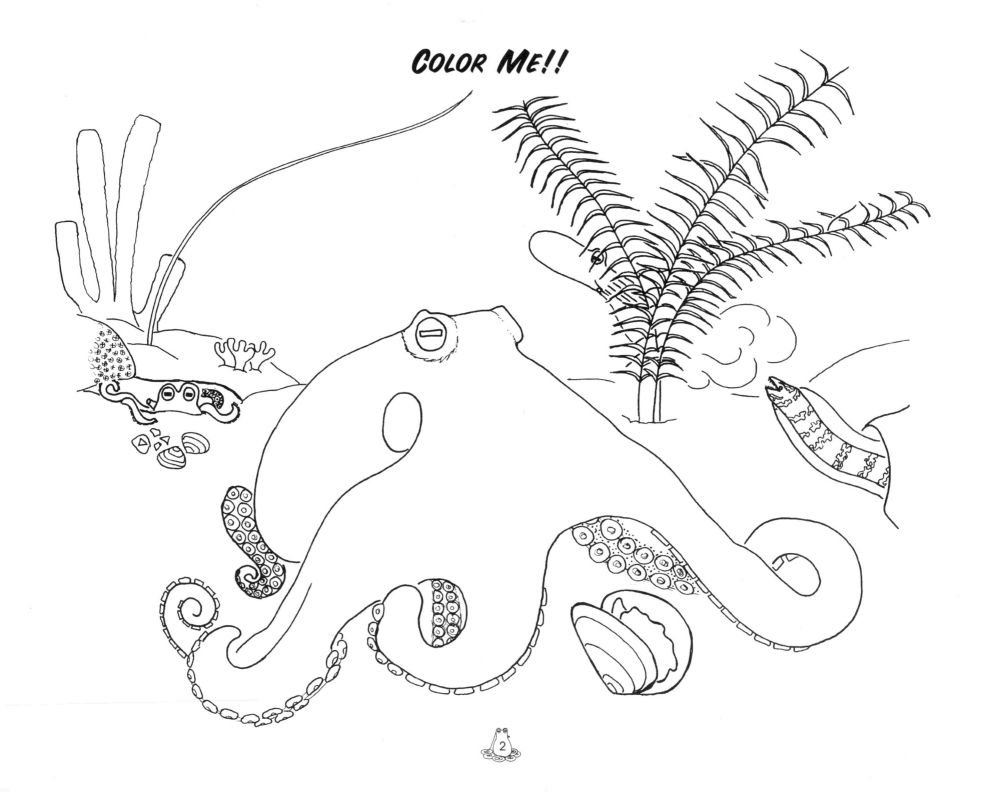

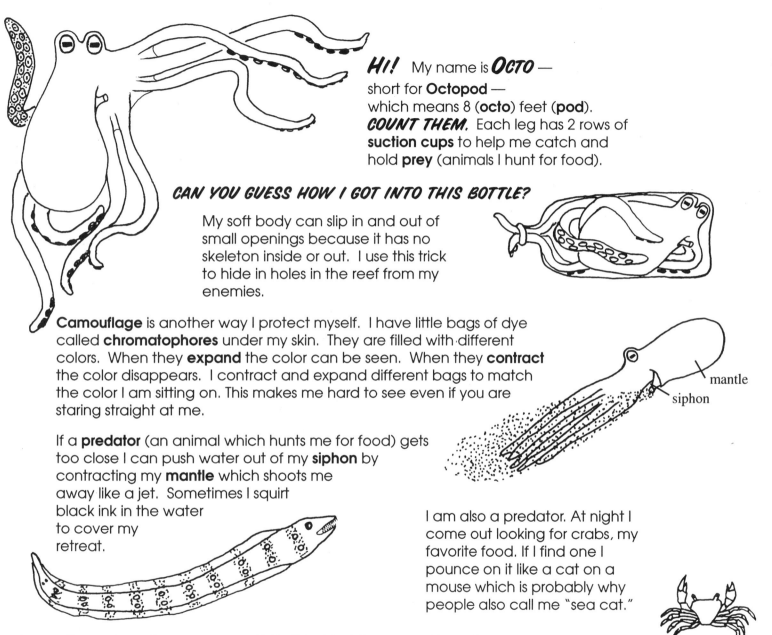

HI! My name is **OCTO** — short for **Octopod** — which means 8 (**octo**) feet (**pod**). **COUNT THEM.** Each leg has 2 rows of **suction cups** to help me catch and hold **prey** (animals I hunt for food).

CAN YOU GUESS HOW I GOT INTO THIS BOTTLE?

My soft body can slip in and out of small openings because it has no skeleton inside or out. I use this trick to hide in holes in the reef from my enemies.

Camouflage is another way I protect myself. I have little bags of dye called **chromatophores** under my skin. They are filled with different colors. When they **expand** the color can be seen. When they **contract** the color disappears. I contract and expand different bags to match the color I am sitting on. This makes me hard to see even if you are staring straight at me.

If a **predator** (an animal which hunts me for food) gets too close I can push water out of my **siphon** by contracting my **mantle** which shoots me away like a jet. Sometimes I squirt black ink in the water to cover my retreat.

I am also a predator. At night I come out looking for crabs, my favorite food. If I find one I pounce on it like a cat on a mouse which is probably why people also call me "sea cat."

I wrap the crab up in my arms and bite it behind the eyes with my **beak** injecting a poison to paralyze it. Clams aren't bad either. I can pull the shells apart using my suction cups. If I find a snail I can either drill a hole in its shell with my beak or wrestle it out of its shell to eat. As you may have guessed I am **carnivorous** meaning I eat meat.

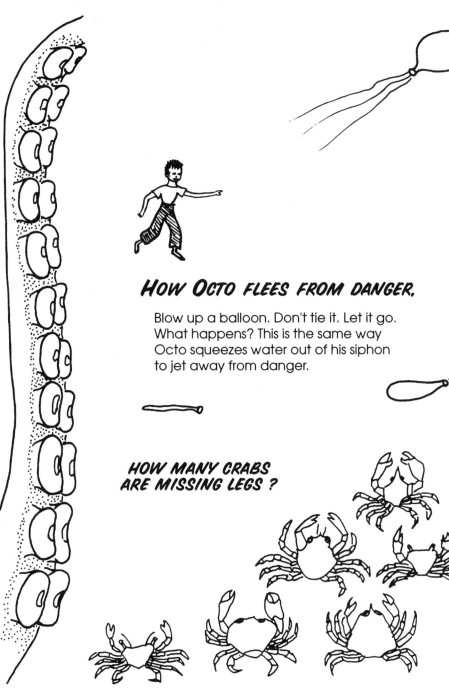

How Octo flees from danger.

Blow up a balloon. Don't tie it. Let it go. What happens? This is the same way Octo squeezes water out of his siphon to jet away from danger.

HOW MANY CRABS ARE MISSING LEGS?

Crossword Puzzle

Words for puzzle are in **bold** on page 3.

Across
1. Animal hunted for food.
5. Dye filled bag which changes size to change an octopus's color.
6. Animal which attacks and kills other animals for food.
7. Action that helps octopuses hold onto things.
8. Part of word that means feet.
9. Part of word that means eight (8).
10. Body of octopus which can contract to force water through the siphon to escape.

Down
2. To spread out getting larger.
3. Tube through which an octopus blows water to jet away when frightened.
4. Meat eating.
5. Blend in with one's surroundings.

Skeletons

Skeletons are made up of hard structures such as shells or bones. They act as frames supporting the soft parts of the body. Skeletons give the body shape—just like the wood in a kite supports and shapes the paper. Because the skeleton is hard it also protects important organs in the body such as the heart.

Imagine what you would look like without a skeleton. Could you stand up and walk around? No! You would be floppy. Muscles attach to skeletons. When they contract they pull on bones. Bones act as levers to move your body.

Some animals, like whales and fish, have skeletons inside their bodies, called **endoskeletons (endo**=inside). Others, like lobsters and conch, have skeletons outside their bodies, called **exoskeletons (exo**=outside). Some have both endo- and exo-skeletons, like sea turtles. Exoskeletons protect animals like suits of armor long ago protected soldiers. Some, like me, have none.

Word Scramble
Unscramble the words below to find out which bones protect these organs.

1. brain — LKUSL _ _ _ _ _ .
2. lungs — BISR _ _ _ _ .
3. spinal cord — RATERBEVE _ _ _ _ _ _ _ _ _ .
4. heart — SIRB _ _ _ _ .

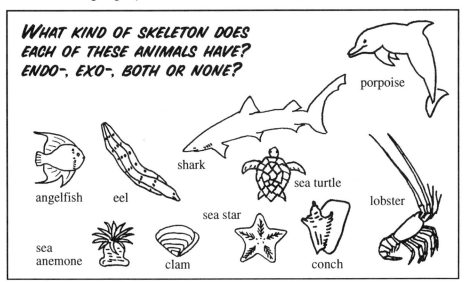

What kind of skeleton does each of these animals have? Endo-, exo-, both or none?

angelfish, eel, shark, sea turtle, porpoise, sea anemone, clam, sea star, conch, lobster

What does this knight in armor have in common with this fish?

WELCOME to my home, the **coral reef**.

Coral reefs are made of limestone, or **calcium carbonate**. Limestone is used to make cement. Your cement houses are built by masons but mine are built by **coral polyps**. Coral polyps are small (ranging from the size of a grain of sand to an EC dollar coin), soft-bodied animals. ***HOW DO SUCH SMALL, FRAGILE BEASTS BUILD THE HUGE REEFS SO MANY ANIMALS CALL HOME?*** By working as a team.

Each polyp builds itself a calcium carbonate exoskeleton for protection. One exoskeleton is hardly noticeable but millions of polyps attach their skeletons together forming a piece of coral, or **coral head**. Coral heads look like large boulders, plates, or "trees" depending on the type of coral polyp that makes them. Brain coral polyps connect to each other in lines forming grooves which look like the surface of a brain. Star coral polyps form separate cups which look like stars.

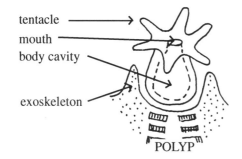

As polyps grow they add more layers to their exoskeletons just like masons add layers of cement blocks to a wall. Only the surface layer of a coral head is living.

There are two types of coral, **hard coral** and **soft coral**. Coral reefs are built largely by hard corals which make exoskeletons as hard as rock. Soft corals have flexible skeletons. Their calcium carbonate is in small spikes, called **spicules.** The spicules are set in a soft gel, so the skeletons can bend.

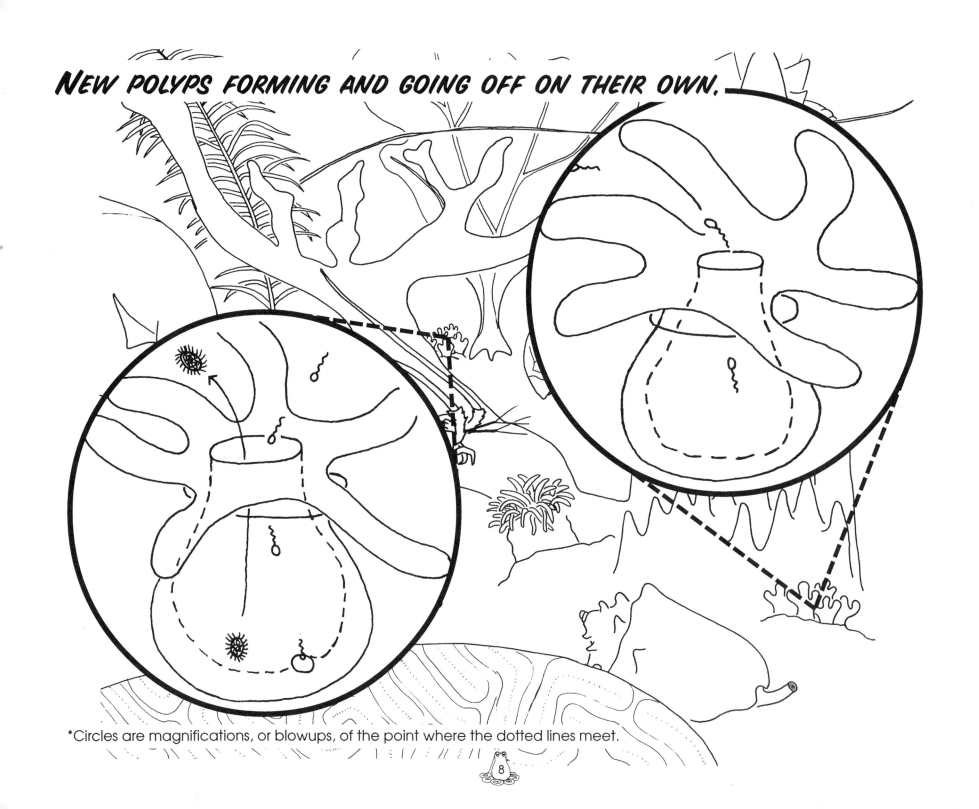

New polyps forming and going off on their own.

*Circles are magnifications, or blowups, of the point where the dotted lines meet.

Come join our team, the Coral Cricketeers!!

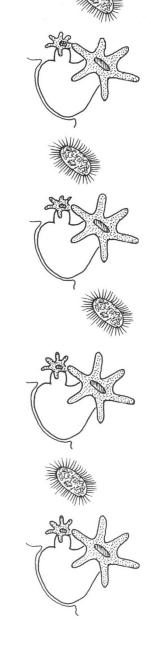

How do coral polyps form the teams that build our reefs? A single coral polyp grows copies of itself. This is called **budding**.

Each bud also forms buds. Eventually teams of coral polyps grow. Each team is called a **coral head**. Every player on a coral head team is **identical** to the first teammate. This is because buds have only one parent. Populations of identical individuals coming from one parent are called **clones**. ***Imagine being able to pinch off copies of yourself to help with your chores!***

BUDDING
(one parent)

Does this mean that all coral polyps come from one parent? No! There is another way to form new **polyps**. Just as you come from a mother and a father, a coral polyp can come from two parents. ***How?*** **Eggs** hang in one parent polyp's body cavity. **Sperm** from other polyps swim into the body cavity through the polyp's mouth. One sperm **fertilizes**, or combines, with one egg to form a **planula**.

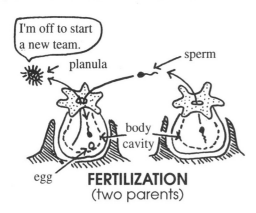

FERTILIZATION
(two parents)

The planula hangs in the body cavity until it is fully developed. Then it breaks loose and swims out through the polyp's mouth. The planula joins the small, floating plants and animals called **plankton**. When a planula is ready, it sinks to the bottom and looks for a clean, hard place to settle. If it finds a good spot, it attaches and turns into a polyp—the ***first teammate***. Each planula is different from all others because it is the combination of two parents.

One-parent polyps **build** reefs.
Two-parent polyps **find new places** to build.

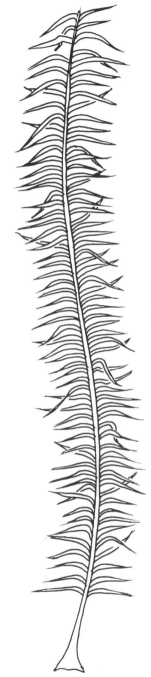

ACTIVITY
WITH THE HELP OF AN ADULT

Dead corals, both hard and soft, often wash up on the beach. Collect a piece of both. Soft coral looks like a fibrous twig. Put each in a separate container and soak them in chlorine bleach. Look at what is left through a magnifying glass.

The gel of the soft coral will dissolve exposing the hard spicules of calcium carbonate in its skeleton. The skeleton of hard coral is solid calcium carbonate. Hard coral might become whiter but the structure will stay the same.

PICK OUT THE IDENTICAL PAIRS.

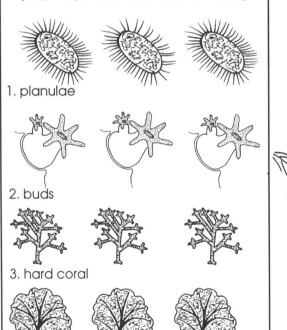

1. planulae
2. buds
3. hard coral
4. soft coral

CORAL IS OFTEN NAMED FOR ITS SHAPE.
Match the names to the numbered corals.
Which are hard corals and which are soft?

Common sea fan
Brain coral
Sea fingers

Pillar coral
Sea feather

Elkhorn coral
Staghorn coral
Devil's sea whip

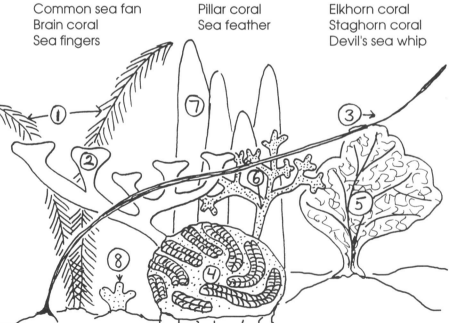

CROSSWORD PUZZLE

Words for puzzle are in **bold** on page 7 and 9.

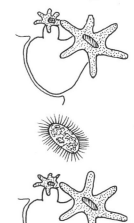

FERTILIZATION MAZE

Help the **star** and **brain** coral sperm (🌀) find eggs (●) of their own kind.

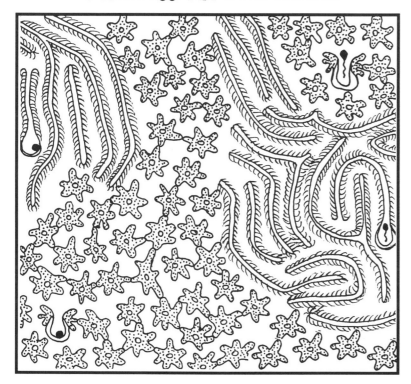

Across
1. Small spikes of calcium carbonate inside soft coral.
6. When a sperm combines with an egg.
8. The way a polyp copies itself, forming a new polyp identical to itself.
10. Small plants and animals which float in the sea water.

Down
2. Free swimming coral individual which has two parents.
3. Female half which is fertilized by a sperm to start a planula.
4. Opening where food and sperm enter polyp and each planula leaves.
5. Exactly alike.
7. Male half that fertilizes an egg to start a planula.
9. Population of identical individuals coming from one parent.

CHECK THIS OUT!!

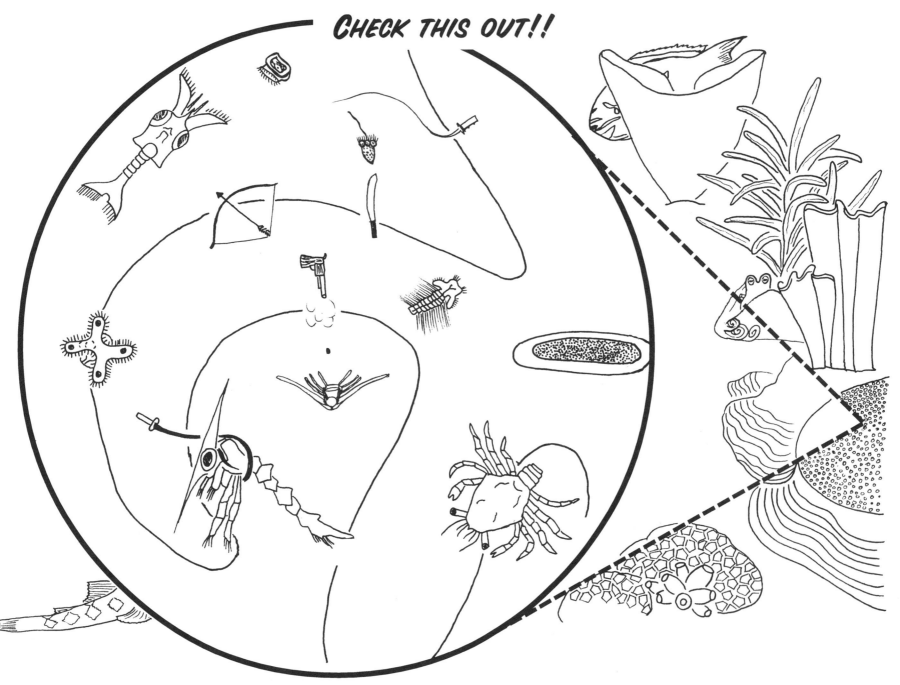

ZOOPLANKTON

CHECK THIS OUT!!

It's a **coral polyp** up close, waiting for food.

Like me, it has arms, called **tentacles,** which wave around its mouth. But the polyp is stuck on its back.
WHO BRINGS IT FOOD? The ocean does.
WHAT DOES THE OCEAN BRING? It brings small, floating animals called **zooplankton**. Baby lobsters, snails, worms and even coral are all part of the zooplankton.
HOW DO POLYPS CATCH ZOOPLANKTON WHEN THEY CAN'T RUN AFTER THEM? They use fancy weapons—darts, whips, and sticky threads. The weapons are on the tentacles. *SEE THE DOTS?* They are called **nematocysts**. Darts inject paralyzing poison into prey. Whips wrap around prey. Sticky threads stick to prey.

Each nematocyst is coiled inside a cell which has a **trigger**. When something touches the trigger, the dart, whip, or sticky thread shoots out, trapping the prey.

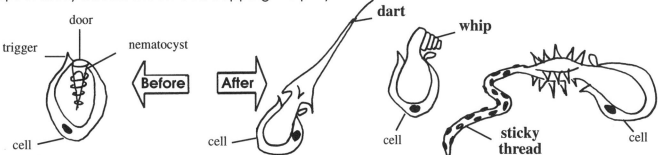

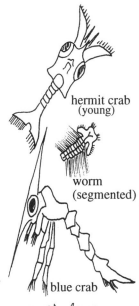

hermit crab (young)

worm (segmented)

blue crab

brittle star

Coral polyps are covered with slimy **mucus**. The mucus helps capture prey and slide it to the mouth. The food is digested in the body cavity.

Living material connects all the polyps on a coral head. Food can pass through the connections after it is digested. *WHAT HAPPENS IF A POLYP DOESN'T CATCH ANY PREY?* Its neighbors share their catch with it through these connections.

Zooplankton is scarce in tropical waters, leaving the sea crystal clear. Coral polyps are such good hunters that more than half the zooplankton is gone after sea water passes over a reef.
SO HOW HAVE THE HUGE CORAL REEFS AROUND OUR ISLANDS GROWN ON SO LITTLE FOOD?

hermit crab (older)

clam (young) (older)

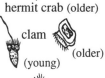

snail

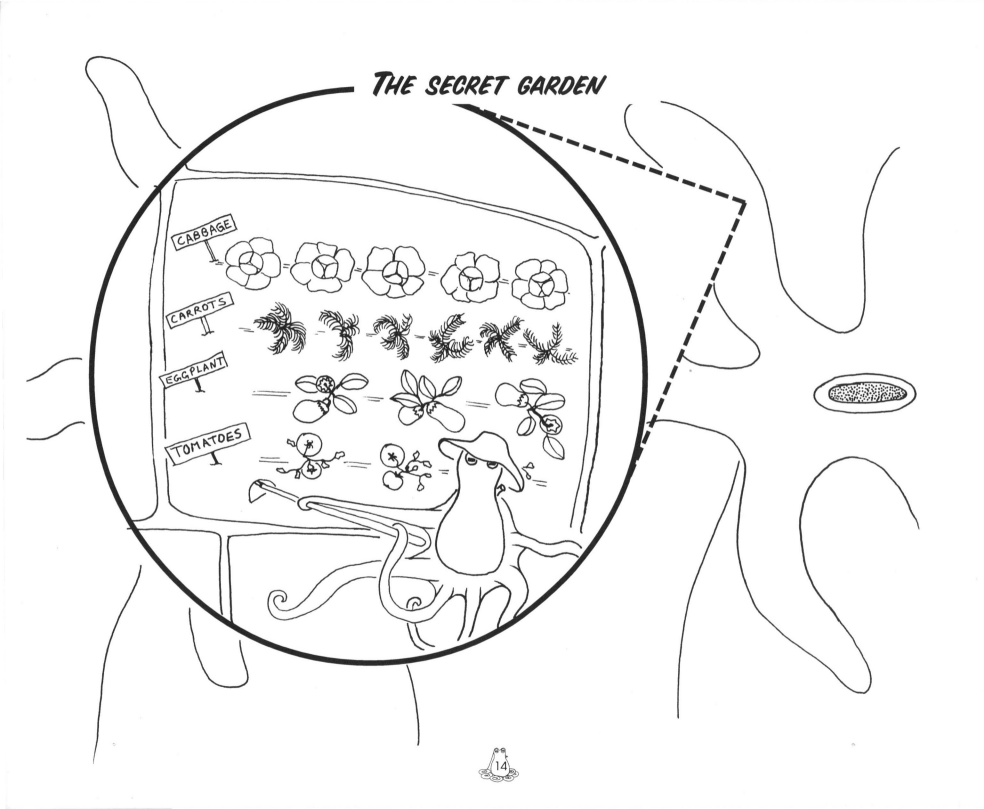

SHERLOCTO the detective and the **Case of the Missing Food.**

Scientists were confused. ***CORAL HAS BEEN VERY SUCCESSFUL BUILDING HUGE REEFS BUT WHERE DOES CORAL GET ENERGY FOR THE JOB?*** Some energy comes from the **zooplankton** that polyps eat. But tropical waters do not have enough zooplankton to feed all the coral. Coral polyps must be eating in secret. ***BUT WHAT?***

———

1,000 zooxanthellae could line up on this line.

Scientists discovered that polyps have a secret vegetable garden inside their bodies. The garden is not like ***OCTO***'s fantasy garden on the facing page. The tiny plants that polyps grow are called **zooxanthellae** (zo zan THEL ee). Zooxanthellae, like other plants, contain **pigments**, or colored chemicals. These pigments catch **sunlight**.

Zooxanthellae use the **energy** from the sunlight to turn waste chemicals from the coral polyp into sugars. This chemical reaction is called **photosynthesis**. The zooxanthellae share the food they make with the polyp. Coral polyps depend on this extra food.

It's a perfect partnership. Zooxanthellae get a safe place to live and chemicals to build sugar. In return, the coral polyps get much needed food.

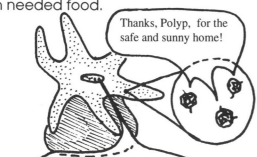

Thanks, Polyp, for the safe and sunny home!

That's all right, Zooxanthellae. You are good guests. I could not live without the extra food you make for me.

The more sunlight zooxanthellae catch, the more food they can make. If the plants do not get enough sunlight to make lots of sugar, the polyps will starve. Sunlight dims as it passes through water. Below 30 feet, 60% of the sunlight is gone. Corals that depend on zooxanthellae must live in shallow water in order for their "vegetable garden" to grow.

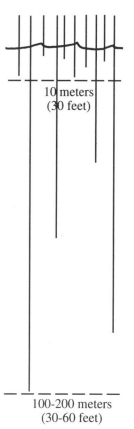

10 meters (30 feet)

100-200 meters (30-60 feet)

How do coral reefs help you?

Unscramble the words in the scene to see how.
How is coral being damaged?

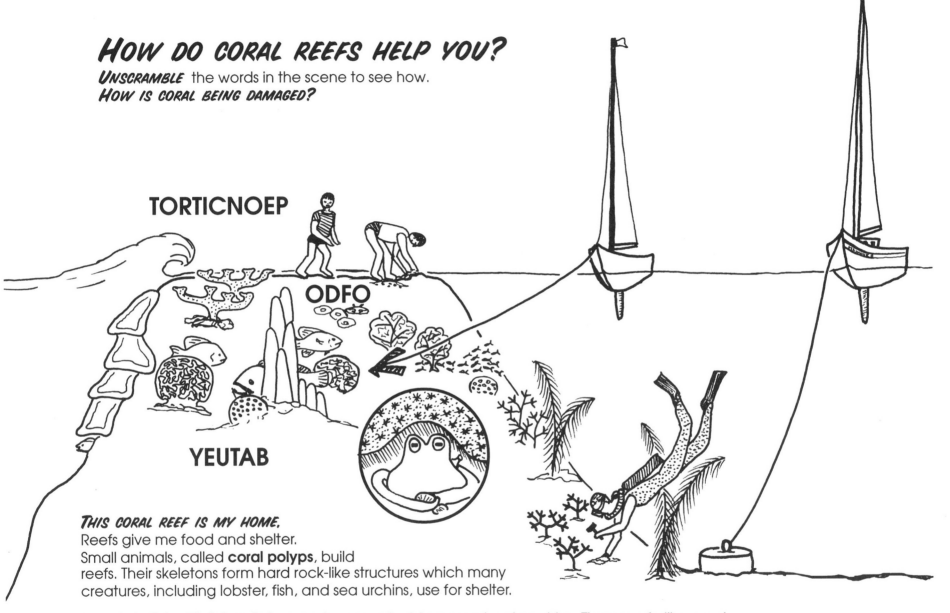

TORTICNOEP

ODFO

YEUTAB

This coral reef is my home.
Reefs give me food and shelter.
Small animals, called **coral polyps**, build
reefs. Their skeletons form hard rock-like structures which many
creatures, including lobster, fish, and sea urchins, use for shelter.

People build **artificial reefs** from rock, cement, old cars and sunken ships. These reefs, like coral reefs, give shelter to animals. **What makes coral reefs different from artificial reefs?** Coral reefs are constantly growing. As the ocean swells and storm surges tear away at the old coral skeletons, polyps replace them. Artificial reefs are not alive. They slowly wear away.

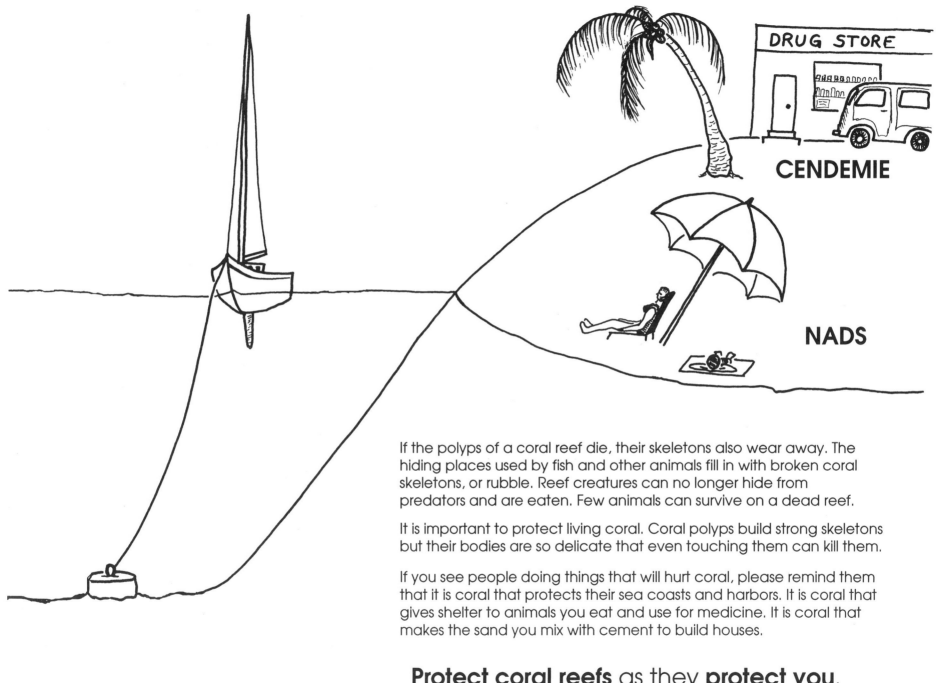

If the polyps of a coral reef die, their skeletons also wear away. The hiding places used by fish and other animals fill in with broken coral skeletons, or rubble. Reef creatures can no longer hide from predators and are eaten. Few animals can survive on a dead reef.

It is important to protect living coral. Coral polyps build strong skeletons but their bodies are so delicate that even touching them can kill them.

If you see people doing things that will hurt coral, please remind them that it is coral that protects their sea coasts and harbors. It is coral that gives shelter to animals you eat and use for medicine. It is coral that makes the sand you mix with cement to build houses.

Protect coral reefs as they **protect you**.

MATCH EACH ZOOPLANKTON LARVA WITH THE ADULT IT WILL TURN INTO.

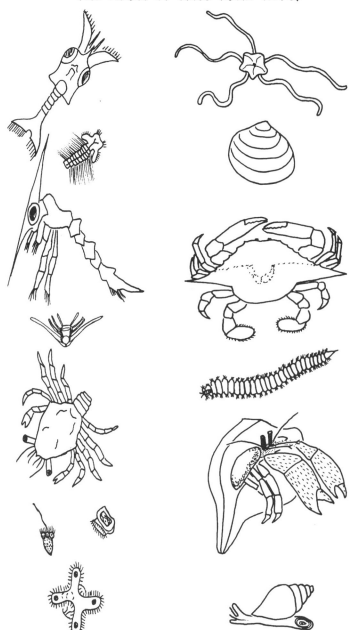

WORD SEARCH

PIGMENT   PHOTOSYNTHESIS
ENERGY   ZOOXANTHELLAE
POLYP   NEMATOCYST
MOUTH   SUNLIGHT
CORAL   PLANKTON
PREY   TENTACLE
DART

```
F T Z C H F Y H D X N D I L N
P H O T O S Y N T H E S I S E
S K O D F R K N P O L Y P O M
U Y X U N H A F E R A C E S A
N D A R T E F L P P T C A R T
L E N E M I R U K I O E I R O
I E T I O A P R E Y G L E R C
G Q H U U R D R I O Y M N E Y
H T E N T A C L E S S E E P S
T E L O H T A D C Y T U R N T
O P L A N K T O N M O V G E T
Y U A O P L A M T C O W Y Q K
P O E Y P D S C V B K H J M A
```

HOW MANY ANIMALS CAN YOU FIND BELOW?

FIND THE ODDBALL.

1. dart nematocysts.

2. ribbon worm babies (part of zooplankton).

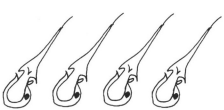
3. coral polyps.

4. whip nematocysts.

5. sticky thread nematocysts.

6. nematocysts before they fire.

"Hush-a-bye baby. Don't you cry."

WORD SCRAMBLE
(based on words from story on page 13.)
Unscramble the letters below. Write the words on the blanks.

1. GURAS   _ _ _ _ _
                    2
2. XNELEZAOTOHAL   _ _ _ _ _ _ _ _ _ _ _
                         3   2   3
3. MIGTEPN   _ _ _ _ _ _ _
                 3   2
4. TESNOOPIHSYTSH _ _ _ _ _ _ _ _ _ _ _ _ _
                           2   2
5. ACLOR   _ _ _ _ _
           2 1
6. GENYRE   _ _ _ _ _ _
              3 3
7. DOFO   _ _ _ _
               3

Now take the letters above the numbers, put them in the spaces below, and unscramble them again.

THE POLYP'S EXTRA FOOD COMES FROM:

_ _ _ _ _ _ _ _ _ _ _ _ .
1 2 2 2 2 2 2 3 3 3 3 3

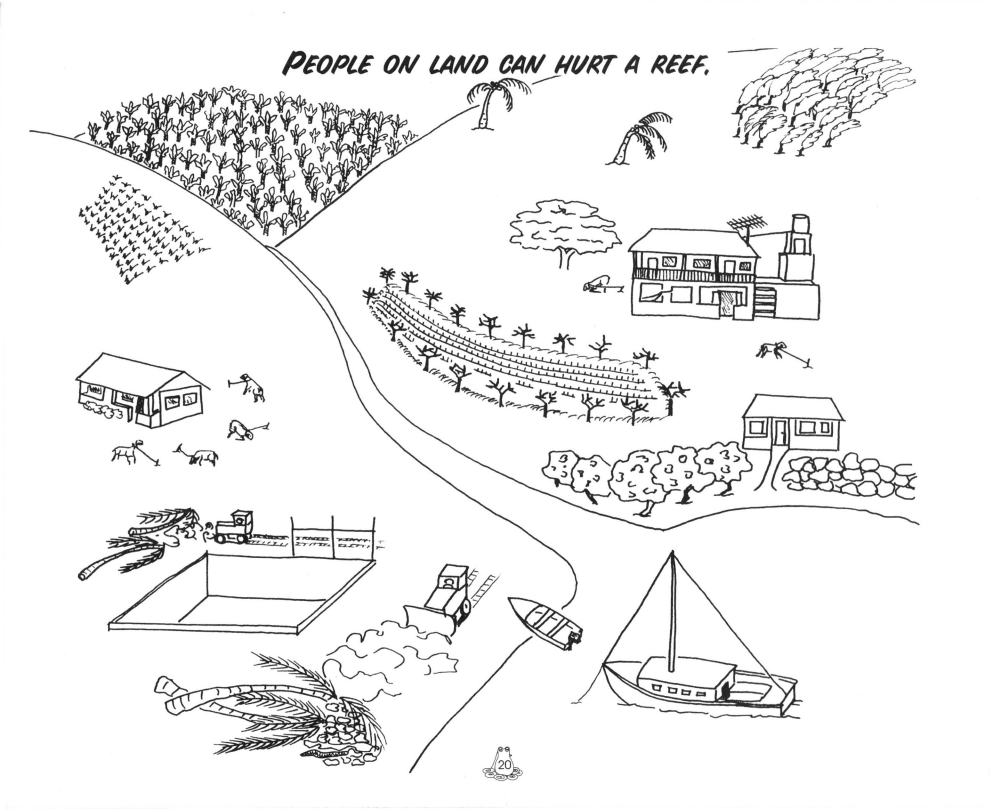

What a mess!! A dirt storm rages around me. My coral home needs sweeping.

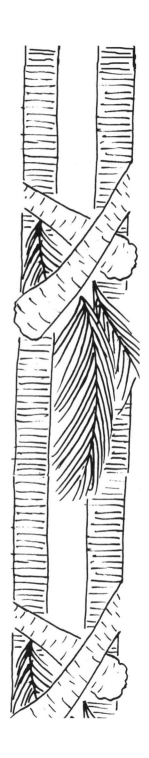

Last night, heavy rain washed **soil** into the sea. Now, even though the sun is shining and the seas are calm it is dark and dirty down here on the coral reef.

Soil is important on land but, in the sea, too much soil causes problems. Small pieces can kill coral polyps. They get stuck in the mucus covering a polyp's tentacles. The soil particles block the polyp's weapons, or **nematocysts**, from catching prey. They shade the tiny plant-like organisms, called **zooxanthellae,** that live inside polyps. Without sunlight, zooxanthellae cannot make food for the polyps. The coral polyps starve.

Years ago less soil washed into the sea. Plants covered the land holding the soil in place. Now, people clear land to grow crops and build houses. They leave the ground bare. Moving water easily picks up the soil and washes it down the hillsides to the sea. This is called **erosion**.

Mangrove swamps form a natural barrier between the land and the reef. Mangrove roots slow the flow of water coming off the land. Soil in the water has time to settle to the bottom of the swamp. **Seagrass beds** also slow down water movement. Where mangroves have been cut down or seagrass beds have been dug up, soil reaches the reef.

What can we do to keep soil from covering coral reefs? Planting trees and borders around crops keeps soil on the land. Replanting forests has slowed erosion on some islands. Coral reefs around these islands are growing back.

Protecting mangrove swamps and seagrass beds also protects coral reefs. Mangroves and seagrasses clean water leaving the land before it reaches the reef.

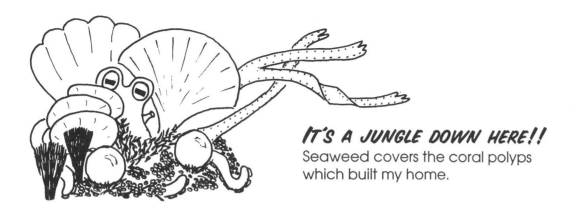

It's a jungle down here!!
Seaweed covers the coral polyps which built my home.

Why is there so much seaweed? **Fertilizers** are helping seaweed grow faster than **grazers** can eat it.

What are fertilizers and where do they come from? Fertilizers are **nutrients**, or food, for plants. Farmers use fertilizers on their crops. When it rains the fertilizers wash into the sea. **Waste,** from **septic systems** and **boats,** as well as **garbage,** such as food scraps thrown into the sea, add to the feast. These may not seem like food to you but they are a treat to seaweed.

What about the grazers? Fewer grazers are on the reef because they have been eaten. People have been **overfishing**. Fish and sea urchins cannot reproduce, or multiply, as fast as people catch them. There are just not enough animals around to trim this seaweed jungle.

Is this jungle a problem? Yes! Coral polyps will die if covered. Coral needs to be clean. Too much seaweed shades the tiny plant-like organisms, called **zooxanthellae**, living in coral polyps. Without sunlight, zooxanthellae cannot make sugar for the polyps to eat.

No new polyps will settle if there are no clean, hard surfaces. Without healthy coral, fish, and urchins will lose the hiding places they depend on for safety. If coral dies it will eventually be worn away by the sea and the land will be left unprotected.

Surprisingly, nutrients, or food, can be harmful to life. If one type of living creature or plant multiplies too fast, other types may suffer. **Balance** is the key. Think of a field grazed by sheep. Too few sheep and the grass grows deep. Too many sheep and the grass will be eaten down to the roots. Neither one is good. A balance between hungry sheep and grass leaves a perfect lawn. The reef is similar. A healthy reef has enough seaweed to feed the fish but not so much that the coral dies.

People must be careful not to upset this balance.!!

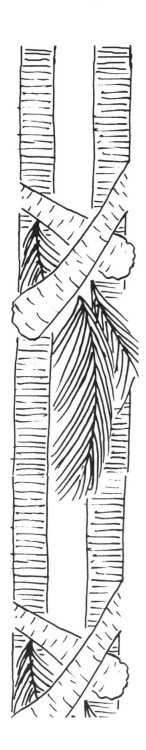

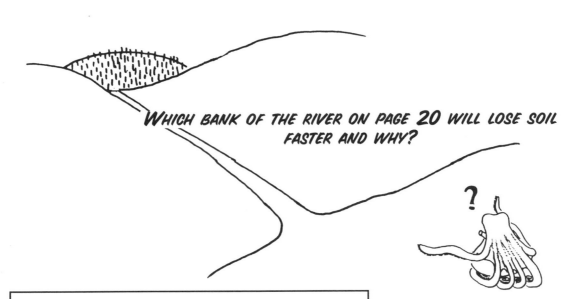

WHICH BANK OF THE RIVER ON PAGE 20 WILL LOSE SOIL FASTER AND WHY?

Is there always dirt in sea water?

After it has not rained for several days wade into the sea beyond the tumbling of the waves. Scoop up some water in a clean container. Pour the water through a coffee filter or a folded paper towel. How does the filter look when all the water has gone through?

After a storm, collect the same amount of seawater in the same way. Pour it through a clean filter. Do the two filters look different? If you don't have a coffee filter or a paper towel, let the container sit over night.

More dirt will be left on the filter from the water following a storm but there is always some dirt in water close to land.

Erosion

Take 2 shallow baking pans. Fill both with dirt to the rim, press it down, and smooth it out. Cover one pan with leaves, twigs, and/or grass. Rest one end of each pan on a piece of wood. Both pieces of wood must have the same thickness so that the pans will be at the same angle. Hold a cup of water one foot above each pan and pour the water along the top edge. Which pan loses more dirt?

Leaf litter protects soil from runoff during rain storms. Less dirt will be lost from the pan with leaf litter on top of the dirt.

Word Scramble

Do you know the reasons for nutrient overload (too much food) in the sea?
Unscramble these words to find out.

ZLIREFTREI   _ _ _ _ _ _ _ _ _ _
                                       =

CPISET MYSSETS   _ _ _ _ _ _   _ _ _ _ _ _ _
                                 =   =

ATBOS   _ _ _ _ _
                                = =

BERAGGA   _ _ _ _ _ _ _
                                     =

RINVIGSFEHO   _ _ _ _ _ _ _ _ _ _ _
                                                  =

What is the key to a healthy environment?

_ _ _ _ _ _ _ _ _ _

Crossword Puzzle

Words for puzzle are in **bold** on page 21 and 23.

Across
3. Catching fish faster than they can reproduce.
6. The key to a healthy environment.
7. Animals which eat algae off the reef.
8. The wearing away of land by moving water.
9. On land plants grow in it. In the sea, coral polyps die when covered by it.
10. Plants that grow underwater and help remove soil from water.

Down
1. Plant-like organisms living in coral polyps.
2. Coral polyps' weapons for catching food.
4. Substances which nourish living things, food.
5. A tree that grows at the ocean's edge and helps remove soil from water leaving the land.

GLOSSARY

OCTOPOD (OCTOPUS) — octo (8) pod (foot). A type of mollusk without a shell.

beak — hard structure surrounding the mouth of an octopus shaped like a parrot's beak.

siphon — tube that allows water to enter and leave the mantle of an octopus.

mantle — body of an octopus that covers its internal organs. When it contracts water shoots out of the siphon jetting the octopus away.

chromatophores — cells on the surface of an octopus filled with pigment. Chromatophores expand (spread out) and contract (pull in) making the octopus's skin change color to match his environment.

suction cups — circular cups which stick to things by creating a suction.

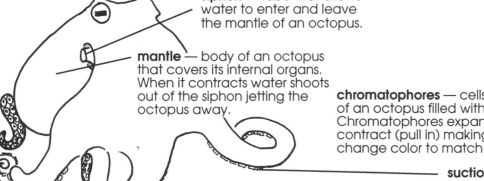

artificial reef — hard structures such as old cars and boats sunk in the ocean. They provide homes for sea animals and hard surfaces for coral polyps to settle on.

balance — to keep in equilibrium or proportion.

budding — a form of asexual reproduction. The parent grows an exact copy of itself.

calcium — chemical found in most skeletons.

calcium carbonate — chemical that makes up coral polyp skeletons. People use it in cement. Also called limestone.

camouflage — to blend in with surroundings.

carnivorous — meat eating.

clone — population of individuals all coming from one parent individual.

coral head — group of coral polyps all coming from the same individual. All the polyps of a coral head are identical.

coral polyp — coral individual. Many growing together make up a coral head.

egg — female germ cell that combines with a similar cell from a male (sperm) to form a new individual by sexual reproduction.

endoskeleton — skeleton inside the body, like a human skeleton.

energy — the capacity to do work.

erosion — wearing away of soil by wind and rain.

exoskeleton — skeleton outside the body like coral polyp skeletons and crab skeletons.

fertilize — when a sperm combines with an egg to form a new individual.

fertilizer — nutrients used to make plants grow better.

grazers — animals which eat algae.

hard coral — coral with an exoskeleton as hard as rock.

identical — exactly the same.

mangrove swamp — group of mangrove trees. Mangroves are trees which can tolerate salt water.

molting — one way animals with exoskeletons grow. They crawl out of their old, hard shell and grow a new, larger one.

mouth of a coral polyp — the opening at the center of the tentacles. Through it food enters the body cavity and waste leaves. Sperm enters the body cavity through the mouth, and planulae leave when they are ready to start a new clone.

mucus — slimy material coating coral polyps that helps the polyp capture prey and slide it to its mouth.

nematocyst — weapon coral polyps use to capture zooplankton for food.

nutrients — something that nourishes living things, food.

overfishing — harvesting fish faster than new ones are produced.

photosynthesis — chemical reaction in which chlorophyll uses sunlight to turn carbon dioxide and water into sugar and oxygen.

overfishing — when fish are caught faster than they can reproduce.

pigments — colored chemicals. Chlorophyll is a pigment which captures the energy in sunlight to be used in photosynthesis.

plankton — living things, both plants and animals, that float in the sea.

planula — the life stage of a coral polyp formed when a sperm from one coral head fertilizes an egg from another coral head of the same type of coral.

predator — animal that hunts other animals for food.

prey — animals hunted for food.

seagrass bed — "field" of grass, such as turtle or eel grass, growing underwater.

septic system — hole in the ground where human waste is put and allowed to break down. Water from the waste filters into the soil.

skeleton — hard structure which hold up a body and gives it shape. Muscles attach to it helping an animal move.

soft coral — coral with a flexible skeleton made up of small spicules of calcium carbonate.

soil — the upper layer of earth in which plants grow.

sperm — male germ cell that combines with a similar cell from a female to form a new individual by sexual reproduction.

spicules — crystals of calcium carbonate in soft corals.

tentacles — "arms" which wave around a coral polyp's mouth.

trigger — small spike on a nematocyst which fires the nematocyst when touched.

waste — whatever is no longer useful.

zooplankton — animals that float in the sea.

zooxanthellae — microscopic (only visible through a microscope) plant-like living things that live inside coral polyp cells and make sugar for the polyp to use.

ANSWERS

From Page 4.

Two crabs are missing legs.

Crossword Puzzle

```
        P R E Y
        X       S           C
        P       I           A
    C H R O M A T O P H O R E
    A   N       H       R
    A       P R E D A T O R
    M       N   O       N
    O           N       I
    S U C T I O N     P O D
      F                 R
      L                 O
    M A N T L E   O C T U
      G                 O
      E                 U
                        S
```

From Page 5.

Word Scramble

1. The SKULL protects the brain.
2. The RIBS protect the lungs.
3. The VERTEBRAE protect the spinal cord.
4. The RIBS protect the heart.

Types of skeletons

porpoise = endo-
shark = endo- (a shark's skeleton is made of cartilage which is not as hard as bone.)
sea turtle = both
eel = endo-
lobster = exo-
angelfish = endo-
conch = exo-
sea star = exo-
sea anemone = none
clam = exo-

WHOOPS! MISSED THAT ONE.

Difference between knight and cowfish.

Humans and fish are both vertebrates. All vertebrates have endoskeletons. A Cow- or "Shell-" fish has a hard shell (exoskeleton) as well, for protection — just like the knight's armor. Therefore they both have exo- and endo- skeletons.

From Page 10.

Identical pairs

1. 1 and 3
2. 2 and 3
3. 1 and 2
4. 1 and 3

Corals

1. Sea feather—soft coral
2. Elkhorn coral—hard coral
3. Devil's sea whip—soft coral
4. Brain coral—hard coral
5. Common sea fan—soft coral
6. Staghorn coral—hard coral
7. Pillar coral—hard coral
8. Sea fingers—hard coral

From Page 11.

Crossword

```
                S P I C U L E
                L       G
              M A N U   G
        I     O   U
        D     U   A
        F E R T I L I Z E S
        N   H   A       P
        T   C           E
    B U D D I N G   C   R
        C           L   M
        P L A N K T O N
        L           N
                    E
```

From Page 16, 17.

PROTECTION
BEAUTY
FOOD
MEDICINE
SAND

Coral is being damaged by people walking on it, a diver with a hammer breaking off souvenirs, and a boat anchored on it.

From Page 18.

In the picture you can find:

school of fish
trumpet fish
moray eel
crab
"Man of War" urchin
white sea egg
brittle star
star fish

shark
jackknife fish
OCTO
jelly fish
fireworm
sea anemone
There are also corals, algae, and a sponge.

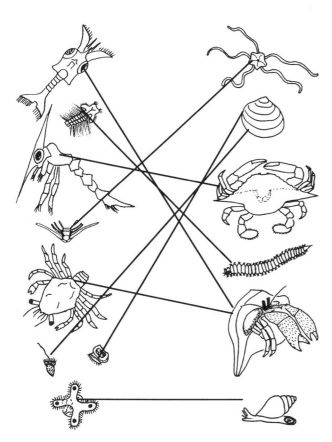

From Page 19.

ODDBALLS

1. Second dart missing spine.
2. First baby has 4 hairs in topknot.
3. Third polyp has 7 tentacles.
4. First whip missing door.
5. Second sticky thread missing nucleus.
6. Third nematocyst missing trigger.

WORD SCRAMBLE

1. sugar
2. zooxanthellae
3. pigment
4. photosynthesis
5. coral
6. energy
7. food

THE POLYP'S EXTRA FOOD COMES FROM:
A SECRET GARDEN

From Page 24.

The left side of the river will lose soil faster because:
1. Bulldozers are clearing the land, removing plants.
2. The sheep are tied too close together and will eat the grass down to bare earth.
3. The garden is not surrounded by a border of plants and the rows are going straight down the hill.

From Page 25.

WORD SCRAMBLE

1. fertilizer
2. septic systems
3. boats
4. garbage
5. overfishing

Key = BALANCE

CROSSWORD PUZZLE

```
        Z
N       O V E R F I S H I N G
E       O           U
M       X   M       T
A   B A L A N C E   R
T       N   N       I
O       T   G   G R A Z E R S
C       H   R       N
Y       E R O S I O N       T
S O I L     V               S
T       L   E
        A
    S E A G R A S S
```

WORD SEARCH

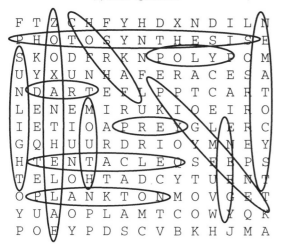

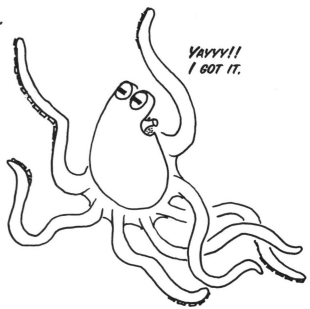

YAYYY!! I GOT IT.

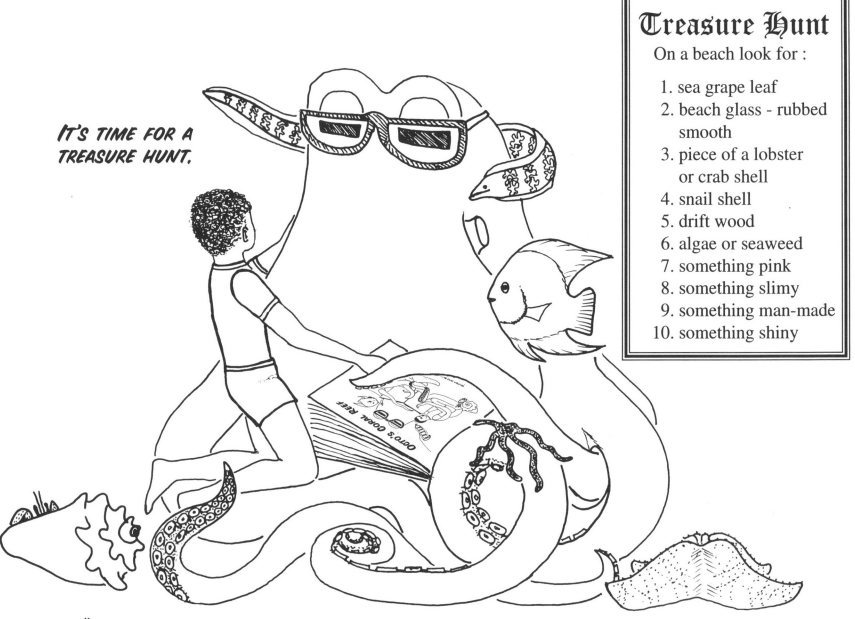

IT'S TIME FOR A TREASURE HUNT.

Treasure Hunt
On a beach look for:

1. sea grape leaf
2. beach glass - rubbed smooth
3. piece of a lobster or crab shell
4. snail shell
5. drift wood
6. algae or seaweed
7. something pink
8. something slimy
9. something man-made
10. something shiny

* Be careful **NOT** to touch any apple-like fruit on the beach. It might be the fruit of the Manchineel tree which is poisonous. If you stand under the tree during the rain you can break out in blisters.

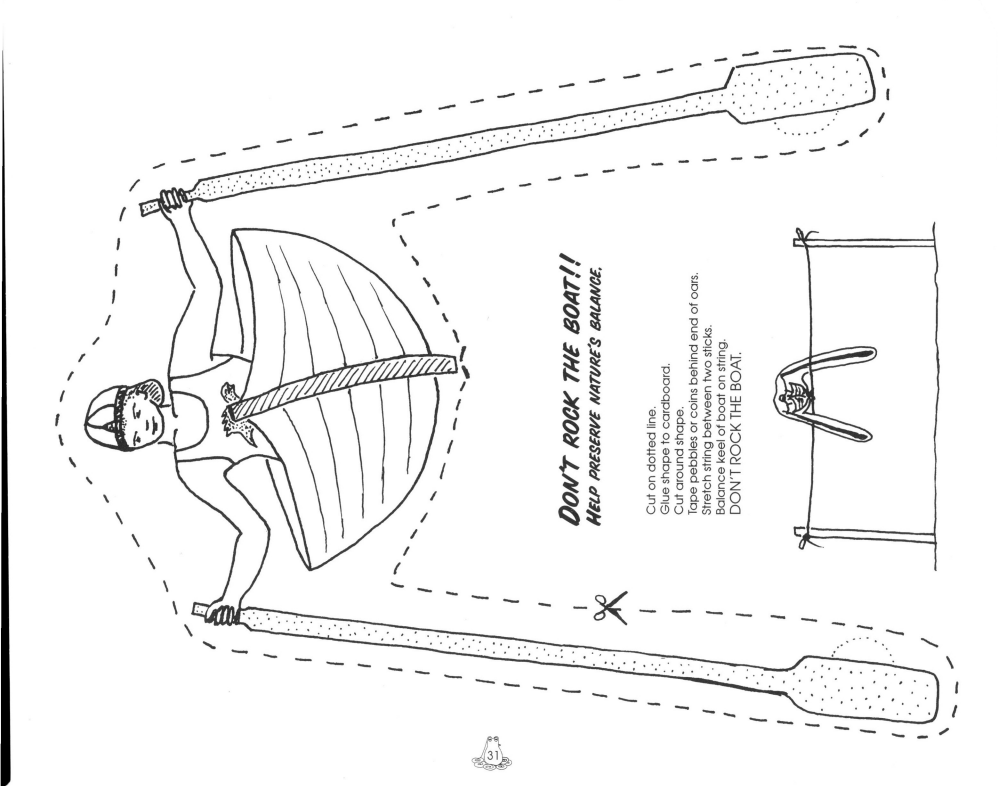